The Listenology Guide
to Bitless Bridles

The Listenology Guide

to Bitless Bridles

Elaine Heney

About Elaine Heney

Elaine Heney is an Irish horsewoman, film producer at Grey Pony Films, #1 best-selling author, and director of the award-winning 'Listening to the Horse™' documentary. She has helped over 120,000+ horse owners in 113 countries to create awesome relationships with their horses. Elaine's mission is to make the world a better place for the horse. She lives in Ireland with her horses Ozzie & Matilda.

Online horse training courses:

Discover our series of online groundwork,
riding & training programs at www.greyponyfilms.com

Enjoy all Elaine's books:

www.elaineheneybooks.com

Table of contents

Introduction to bitless bridles 9

What do the horses think? 18

10 Reasons to go bitless 20

Benefits of a bitless bridle 21

Bitless bridle styles 23

Choosing the right bitless bridle 24

Bitless bridle checklist 26

#1 Bitless bridle for advanced riding 27

Global bitless bridle issues 29

Groundwork is critical 37

Groundwork exercises 39

Changing your riding cues 40

Types of bitless bridles - Rope halter 42

Types of bitless bridles - Sidepull 46

Types of bitless bridles - Cross-under and cross-over 48

Types of bitless bridles - Hackamore (Jacuima) 51

Types of bitless bridles - Mechanical hackamore 56

Bitless bridle problems to avoid 58

Benefits of using a rope halter 60

Benefits of using a hackamore 61

12 reasons people use a bosal & mecate 62

Should you try riding bitless? 68

Rope halter success stories 78

Bitless bridle success stories 82

Hackamore success stories 92

Final thoughts 97

You did it... 102

Introduction to bitless bridles

Choosing to ride bitless can happen for many different reasons. Perhaps you have a horse that seems unhappy when ridden with a bit. Or you are interested in the California Vaquero tradition. Or perhaps you've seen someone riding in a bitless bridle and you are curious. Or maybe you just thought it was something that you'd like to try with your horse.

There are definitely some things to take into consideration before you decide if you should try a bitless bridle with your horse, and which bridle would work best for you. This guide will cover a lot of useful information and help you choose your new bridle and start riding bitless.

Rope halters in New Zealand

I stumbled into the world of riding bitless by accident. I went backpacking to Australia & Zealand in my early twenties. After two months of living out of a suitcase, I decided to start looking for a horse job. Up to this point I had not really seen anyone ride bitless, so riding without a bit was not on my radar at all.

I sent emails to a lot of horse treks in Australia & New Zealand, looking for a job. One horse trek centre in the South Island in New Zealand, emailed me back with a job offer. They needed a trail guide for their trek business, bringing tourists on horseback around the Southern Alps. I would work a few hours every day in exchange for room and board. It sounded perfect! I had no idea what type of horses they had, how they were trained or what tack they were using.

I booked a flight from Brisbane and arrived over two days later. I had ridden horses since I was young, and I loved horses a lot. However, some bad experiences getting lessons when I was a teenager had made me believe that advanced flatwork, dressage, lateral work and collection were only possible if you were quite rough on your horse. A lot of getting horses to look 'collected' involved very heavy hands, a lot of leg pressure and a lot of pulling on the reins.

I had a few lessons where it was suggested that I needed to apply some heavy handed tactics to get the right head position so my horse would look collected. And extra bits were suggested too.

None of that sat right with me. So I retired from exams & competitions and resigned myself to doing my own thing.

When I arrived in New Zealand, the horses at the horse treks were beautifully cared for. They lived together in a beautiful pasture at the foot of the mountains. And to my astonishment, all of these horses, from a 12.2 pony to a 17h Clydesdale cross were ridden in rope halters and not a bit in sight, all around the mountains.

At that stage, I had never seen a rope halter in my life! And I had certainly never considered using only a rope halter to take out tourists, many of whom had never ridden a horse before. Seeing these beginner riders ride these horses all over the mountains safely without a bit amazed me. I had never seen anything like it back in Ireland. Over the three months I was there, all the tourists were safe and happy. All the horses were happy and healthy. And it was a wonderful place to work.

One of the trail guides was a friend of mine called Cathy. She rode a beautiful chestnut horse. One day I saw Cathy riding her chestnut horse in a rope halter around the top paddock. But instead of attaching the lead rope to the halter to make the normal two reins, she had hopped on her horse bareback and was riding with the lead rope as one rein. But she wasn't just walking along on the horse, bareback and in a halter.

Cathy was cantering her chestnut horse, bareback, in perfect circles, with a soft bend through her horse's body, in a rope halter with one rein. Her horse was totally relaxed and completely collected. The horse's hind quarters were engaged, the core muscles were engaged, the horses back had lifted a little, the withers had lifted and the poll was the highest point of the horse's body. My previously held belief that collection was only something that could be achieved with force and pressure - was completely shattered.

Not only could collection be achieved in a kind way, but you it looked like you didn't need a saddle. You didn't need a bit either. You didn't need to pull on any reins. Tough leg pressure was not needed either. And if you wanted to, you only needed one rein!

It was like my whole world shifted 180 degrees. A new path to incredible horsemanship - that was kind to the horse, without using any force or gadgets - had just appeared in front of me.

A few months later, I flew home with a new mission. That mission was to restart my horsemanship education, using gentle and kind ways to work with horses and to begin riding in one of these astonishing rope halters. Could I get the same results with my horses?

Ozzie the Connemara goes bitless

I bought Ozzie my Connemara, when he was five years old in Kilkenny, Ireland. I spent a few months doing groundwork in a rope halter. This was the same type of rope halter that I had seen work so well in New Zealand. I started him under saddle in just a halter, and we rode for quite a few years in a rope halter. It worked fine for us.

I used a bit just two or three times with Ozzie - just in case he ever in his life needed to be ridden with a bit by someone else - which seemly sensible but unlikely.

Ozzie understood how the halter worked because of the groundwork exercises we did with it. Developing a horse to be soft, light and collected in just a halter totally fascinated me. When going down this path, in hand work is an important part of the foundations.

Back in Australia, my friend Steve Halfpenny had started to ride his horses in California hackamores (bosal & mecate). This was a direct influence on the clinics he hosted with Jeff Sanders from California. Steve appreciated Jeff's view that horsemanship is an art form.

A California hackamore is basically a nose band made from rawhide (this is called the bosal), a strip of leather that goes from the over the top of the horse's head to keep the bosal on, and then the reins are a long handmade rope made from horsehair, that you attach to the bosal. There is no bit. There is another type of hackamore that relies on poll pressure. This bosal and mecate setup does not use poll pressure.

As a California hackamore doesn't move around on the horse's face like a rope halter does, the signal is more clear and consistent for the horse. This is super important when you are working on subtle cues and high level riding manoeuvers.

If you're not familiar with a bosal and mecate you do first need to learn about them. You don't just put one on your horse and ride off into the sunset! The first time I saw the hackamore (bosal and mecate) I felt overwhelmed. It seemed complicated. How would you know which size to get or how to know it was handmade correctly? Once you buy it, how to fit and shape it to your horse? And how on earth do you tie the mecate reins to the bosal? There is a very specific knot to use.

So the first time I was introduced to someone riding with a bosal and mecate, I didn't jump in straightaway to change from my halter. But I suspected it would be in my future when I was ready for it and wanted to progress further with smaller cues, that what was I currently using riding in a rope halter.

About two years later, I was ready for the hackamore. I understood that it would make it easier for Ozzie to understand me, with more refined signals. I researched the best places to get one by asking friends who had been taught by Steve & Jeff. I learned how to fit them, and how to shape them. I even learned how to tie the reins! It's like anything, once you figure it out it's quite easy. I have been riding Ozzie now for over five years in a hackamore. It is great for both of us and I would never change it.

Then a new horse came into my life.

I bought Matilda, a bay Irish sports horse as an unstarted five year old. We did about eight weeks of groundwork in a rope halter to begin with, to prepare her for the backing process.

Her first few rides were in a rope halter. While she was very soft & had a lovely bend through her body on the groundwork, from the first day I sat on her back there was no bend in her body.

She was like a plank of wood. There was no bend in her neck whatsoever! When I asked for a gentle bend at a walk, it was not available. Not having the bend meant that I couldn't do an emergency stop if I needed it (turning your horse in a small circle to slow them down), so it wasn't very safe.

As she had no steering while I was riding her, I put her in a bridle and a bit for a few weeks. The first time I put it in her mouth she was curious and it was no problem. The second time I took out the bridle and bit, she turned her head away from me. So she didn't like it.

As she still had no steering or bend though her body, for safety I rode her in walk, with very gentle hands for a few weeks. To help her to learn I was very careful to only use one rein when I needed it and then release it again. Each day she would get a little softer and a little more bend would become available. This meant that we were getting safer.

After a few weeks, when I had a bend through her body on a circle in both directions, backup was excellent and I could ask her to turn her neck left and right in walk and trot, I stopped using the bridle. I decided switched to a California hackamore.

I would have preferred if she had been soft in her body from the first day and I never had to use a bit but I am happy that I put safety first, and only switched to the hackamore when I had done enough preparation for us to be successful with it.

It's worth bearing in mind that there is no one correct bridle (bitted or bitless) that suits all horses. And that sometimes at different stages of our horses development, we might need to change to a different bridle that would better suit our situation. One situation that often comes up is the need to be able to ride with a bit for some competitions.

We want to use the best bridle that will help our horse's to understand our signals and that fits them perfectly, causes no harm and also fits the situation we are in.

Matilda is now a joy to ride in a hackamore. She is the bay mare you may have seen in the Trail Brave course and some of Steve Halfpenny's online lessons that were filmed in Ireland.

For me, I want to be constantly improving my riding skill, lightness, softness, collection and lateral work. The hackamore is a tool which has historically been proven to be able to help people achieve this goal with their horses.

What do the horses think?

Are horses happier in bitless bridles? It's certainly an interesting question. For some horses who have the perfectly fitted bit and a rider with kind & sensitive hands, they may be equally comfortable in both. Some horses do dislike particular types of bitless bridles. Some don't like the restriction of cross under bridles, or the poll pressure on mechanical hackamores, so you could argue they would also prefer a bit.

I asked horse riders in our Listening to the Horse community, who had transitioned to bitless riding this question, to better understand their horse's experience.

96.2% of all bitless riders surveyed said their horse was happier in a bitless bridle, compared to a bit.

One significant issue with bits today is that we have lost the art of fitting a bit. At clinics with Jeff Sanders he talked about people who would travel around fitting bits, and even making them.

They were experts on the anatomy of the horse's mouth and how to take that into account when sorting out a bit for them. The good news is that, with so much more interest in making things right for horses, professional bit fitters are emerging again today. The bad news however is that it is still the case that most bits are chosen not based on the horse's individual mouth confirmation, but because it was recommend as a 'kind bit' in a tack shop, or as a 'good bit' by a friend who uses it on their horse (who likely has a totally different mouth anatomy), or even as more severe option for control.

10 Reasons to go bitless

I asked over five hundred bitless riders in the Listening to the Horse community what is the main reason they like using a bitless bridle (or rope halter or hackamore) when riding their horses. Here are some of their replies:

- My horse likes it more than using a bit. He is more relaxed, calm, light, responsive, happier and softer. He doesn't pull or head shake or clench his jaw any more.
- I like how the bridle is not close to my horse's eyes.
- I like not having metal in horses' mouths.
- My horse can eat and drink more easily on long rides without a bit in his mouth.
- I like my bitless bridle as the leather is soft & good quality.
- A bitless bridle is good for inexperienced riders, as there is less chance of hurting the horse's mouth. It's also easier for kids to learn.
- I like my bitless bridle as it looks like a traditional English bridle.
- With a bitless bridle, there is no bit to warm up in cold weather.
- My bitless bridle makes me a better rider. I now use my hands less and my body cues more.
- I like my bitless bridle as my horse is able to yawn and lick and chew.

Benefits of a bitless bridle

Since I filmed the docu-series 'Listening to the Horse', I have got lots of emails from people who are fascinated by the concept of riding a horse without a bit.

There are many advantages to riding without a bit for the horse and for the rider. I was curious to know which reasons resonated the most with our community. So I asked our community what was the main reason they were interested in riding without a bit. Here are some of their responses.

- There is more relaxation, and it is more comfortable for the horse. I think it is kinder and gentler for the horse.
- There is less potential pressure or pain caused inside the mouth. I don't like the idea of controlling a horse using metal in their mouth.
- The bit irritates my horse. He chews it, head tosses, hates being bridled, his tongue goes over the bit, my fidgets, head shakes, pulls, has a busy mouth and over flexes.
- Riding bitless works better for a horse with a sensitive mouth.
- Riding bitless offers better communication.
- My horse has teeth issues, so most bits cause an issue.

- Mouth anatomy issues - from not too much room for a bit to injuries and melanomas.
- My horse had a bad experience with bits previously.
- Riding bitless can improve the rider's skills, and help the rider to stop pulling.
- A bitless bridle helps to avoid the 'which bit is ok' guesswork.
- With a bitless bridle it is easier for the horse to graze.
- Green riders won't pull on horses' mouths by accident.
- If a horse has wolf teeth in the way of a bit, bitless can solve this issue.
- Previous injury or nerve damage to the head, can mean a bit will not be suitable. So a bitless bridle would be useful.

Bitless bridle styles

I've divided the different types of bitless bridles into five categories:

- **Rope halters & headcollars:** These are any type of halter or headcollar that is used for riding.
- **Sidepulls:** With these you attach the reins to each side, thus the name 'sidepull'. These won't tighten on the face or exert poll pressure.
- **Mechanical hackamore:** These have some sort of metal attachment on the noseband, which the reins are attached to. When you apply contact to the reins it gives a cue to move the head sideways. The leverage also puts pressure on the poll of the horse.
- **Cross overs:** The reins are connected to some form of strap that crosses under the jaw. When contact is applied to the reins, part of the bridle tightens around the horse's face.
- **The California hackamore**: This is a traditional tool, originally brought from Spain to Mexico & California. The noseband (bosal) is made from rawhide or similar soft leather, and the reins (mecate) are made traditionally from horse hair.

We will discuss each category in more depth in upcoming chapters, to help you to make the right decision for your horse.

Choosing the right bitless bridle

With five different bitless bridle types, and then a huge amount of varieties and brands in each type (except the California hackamore, that must be made a specific way and adhere to the traditions) it can be overwhelming to start to figure out the best type to try out with your horse.

A good place to start is to identify your goals.

Your goals:

Do you really want to improve your flatwork and riding, are you happy hacking out and just enjoying the ride or something else? Do you have time to learn a new tool that will improve your riding skills? For higher level performance the California hackamore could be the tool for you. For hacking you might decide on a sidepull or one of the other options.

Your training method:

Think about what fits in with your current training, cues & methods. For example, if the bridle causes poll pressure, it would not be suitable if you've taught your horse to lower head when touched on the poll.

Importance of instant release:

Consider whether instant release is important to you. The ability to have great timing using an instant release when training your horse makes it much easier for your horse to learn. Bear in mind that cross under bridles and scrawbrigs are not designed to be used for riding in a constant contact and will be uncomfortable for your horse if you do.

Tiny cues and more advanced riding:

Think about whether you want subtle, refined communication and precise signals to your horse or if that is not so important to you. Think about the difference in signals between a rope halter and California hackamore, for example.

Competitions:

Do you want to compete? Some organising bodies do not accept bitless bridles in their competitions.

Bitless bridle checklist

As a brief recap on some of the information previously discussed, here are some key points to consider when you choose your bitless bridle:

- Ideally does not use any/much poll pressure
- Does not move around a lot (to avoid giving your horse inconsistent signals)
- Quick release (there can be issues with the cross under design)
- I will not ride with a constant contact (especially with cross under bridles and bosals). Sometimes if you are used to riding with constant contact, you'll need to fix your patterns and muscle memory.
- With a bitless bridle your horse is able to open his mouth and yawn widely, can lick his lips, eat, drink with no bit in the way, and without their mouth being tied shut.
- Any bridle (bitless or otherwise) needs to be made of high quality material. Often cheaper tack, uses lower quality materials and often the standard of workshop is not great – which can lead to the equipment rubbing or hurting your horse when you use it.
- What are your personal riding goals? Do the events or competitions you go to allow any type of bitless bridles? If they do not currently, have you asked someone if they would consider it?

#1 Bitless bridle for advanced riding

When I saw my friend Cathy and her chestnut horse doing beautiful collection in a rope halter that day in New Zealand, it was clear to me that my riding goal was to aim for the most advanced and subtle riding skills I could attain.

With various different types of bitless bridles to choose from, I thought it would be interesting to ask current bitless riders in our community what they thought was the best type of bitless bridle for this goal. So I asked the question:

"Which bitless bridle is the best if your goals are advanced horsemanship, collection, lateral work and developing your horsemanship to an art form level?"

And here are the answers:

- 46.4% of those surveyed said if fear, lack of suitable education, and money were not issues for you, a California hackamore would improve your level of horsemanship & riding the most and allow you to develop your riding into an art-form.
- 22% said a side pull bridle.

- 17.9% said a rope halter.
- The remainder said a mechanical hackamore or crossunder bridle.

Global bitless bridle issues

Finding the correct bitless bridle is not always an easy option. Here are some stories of issues that have been encountered from horse riders around the world.

Cross-under issues:

- *"I have avoided the bitless bridles that cross under the chin. I've been told they don't give immediate release of pressure."*
- *"I have used cross under with my previous horse but with my current horse I felt it wasn't quick enough release and was a bit confusing."*
- *"I ride with a side pull. I have found that other bitless bridles don't release pressure quick enough or not at all, with the side pull I don't have this problem. In the side pull my horses respond quickly to a soft request."*
- *"I hated the bitless bridle. I tried. Its design made my horse claustrophobic. It applied so much pressure under the jaw and chin from it's criss/cross rein design that squeezed the horses face. I would never recommend this design."*
- *"I ride with a California hackamore now. I've tried a cross under bitless bridle, and my horse greatly disliked it as the release of pressure isn't fast enough. The flat rein*

attachments don't slide well through the round rings which causes a delay in pressure release.

- "I have ridden in a cross under bitless bridle quite a bit. It is not great for shaping the horse because there is not an immediate release and the direction of the pressure is off.

- I started out with the cross under styles, which seemed to work fine at first, but my horses did not seem to like all the strapping on their heads and also the poll pressure those can generate. The rule seems to be less is more for me."

- The crossover bitless really confused my horse."

- "I took my bitless bridle back because I thought it might be too severe around the nose."

- "I have a leather bridle that was designed to work with pressure, it had two straps crossed under the chin that you connect the reins to, but they didn't release very well after application."

- "I tried a cross under bitless bridle once and all of my horses hated it. I feel they objected to the restrictive nature of it. It over communicated with pressure or in places they just aren't accustomed to."

- "I have tried the nose band that tightens, and squeezes the nose. My mare didn't like this pressure and there is an issue of not having an instant release of pressure.

- "Flower hackamores tend to flip upside down - I've corrected this by adding an extra connecting chin strap. I've found that cross under styles such as indian hackamore (especially rope ones) tend to stick and don't release quickly enough. I no longer use these and don't recommend them. The cross under bridle is slightly better but again with a rider with heavy hands, or if you ride with a constant contact, it gives the horse no escape or relief."

Sidepull issues:

- "When using a padded English side pull style (no cross under) I found it would shift a fair amount unless it was much tighter than I would prefer."
- "I ride in a bitless bridle I designed myself and while I'm happy with it I would like to move into a California hackamore. Features of my bridle that I like are a curved crown piece that doesn't press up against the ears, cheek pieces that sit well clear of the eyes, a simple but strong rein ring attachment and good overall stability on the horse's head. It's great for general trail riding but there's not much finesse so I'm looking forward to the hackamore."
- I tried a leather one which was very tight across the nose and browband. Also extremely hard to get on and off."

Mechanical hackamore issues:

- "I've ridden with a mechanical hackamore that my horse seemed to prefer over a bit, but it was still too easy to put too much pressure (due to my inexperience) which resulted in her rearing once. No injuries, but it taught me a good lesson."
- "I do not like a "bitless" that uses a long shank, an English hackamore...put one across your shin and secure it... give it a pull and see how you like it.. you won't."

- *"I am not too fond of any mechanical hackamores. I have only tried a flower hack once; it felt too severe to me. Also you need to attach it to your horse's head pretty tightly so that it won't slip, when riding. So in my opinion even at rest the horse doesn't have as much room as it does for example with a sidepull or rope halter."*

Rope halter issues:

- *"I used to ride in a rope halter, but now I find it crude and ineffective. I would not choose to go back to it except in an emergency."*
- *"I have ridden in a rope halter and a regular halter. Both seem to not have a good enough fit."*
- *"I sometimes ride in a rope halter but it's just not accurate enough for training."*
- *"Yes I've tried different rope side pulls and didn't like the nose band as they moved too far across the face, the chin straps were too long."*
- *"I have tried a cross under. I found that it did not release pressure quickly enough. I have also ridden with a halter but they slip around too much on a horse's face so I would not go for a long ride using a halter."*

Cheap bitless bridles:

- *"I got a cheap bitless bridle. I had to modify it to not bunch near his eye even with slight reins pullback."*

- *"The deterioration of the material in my cross under bridle prevented the reins from sliding through the rings, which caused an issue."*
- *"When I first transitioned to bitless I just bought a super cheap one for £30. It was inflexible and I don't feel that it put pressure in the correct places."*
- *"Any California hackamore with a cable core. Garbage."*
- *"I tried a webbing one and it was awful. No substance to the webbing and it twisted badly."*
- *I tried a bitless bridle but it sat too close to my horse's eye and twisted on his face, however, it fits my daughter's horse nicely. So head shape can impact fit.*

Common bitless bridles issues

It's not all perfect with bitless bridles. There are some challenges that bitless riders may come across. I surveyed hundreds of bitless bridle riders and asked what their challenges are while riding bitless.

52% of all bitless riders have no issues with their bitless bridle, halter or California hackamore. Of the 48% of bitless riders who shared an issue, these were the biggest issues they encountered while riding bitless.

- My bitless bridle is not competition legal 9.8%
- I do not like the comments from other riders 7.5%
- I do not know if it is fitted correctly 5.5%
- I have some stopping and slowing down issues 5%
- I feel afraid (but my horse is fine) 3%
- I need to learn how to help my horse become more collected when we ride 3%
- I am not happy with the crossunder release 3%
- My horse eats grass 2.5%
- I need to do more groundwork 2.5%
- The bitless bridle is too close to eye 1.6%
- I'm worried about control in extreme situations 1.6%
- It's hard to find a local bitless trainer 1%
- Riding with a bitless bridle is not covered by my insurance 1%
- I bought a poor quality hackamore that I can't use 1%

Here are some of their thoughts:

Don't forget to do groundwork first.

"I think some people would try bitless but expect to go straight from a bit to bitless without any ground work to show the horse how he should behave with one. This causes a lot of problems and puts people off because of the lack of experience from others trying it."

Faith may be required.

"I think for most people it is a fear, they feel the bit gives them control, a leap of faith is required. The horse competition world is to blame too. For dressage a double bridle is required! If a horse can understand and is good enough in a bitless it shouldn't matter."

Take care of the situations you put yourself and your horse into.

"Of course if you have always ridden with a bit it is scary at first to go bitless. Especially if you don't really know the horse. But really a bit isn't going to stop a bolting horse either. Get the training right then trust the horse. Don't put your horse into a situation that would result in a bolt."

Get some groundwork lessons!

"I used to think that a strong bit is needed for control but after a horse took off with me despite having a pretty strong bit I realized it was more about groundwork."

Groundwork is critical

Riding is not all just about bitless bridles & tack. It's more so about our partnership with our horse, and how well educated our horses are to ride.

Putting a new device on your horse's head is not going to be a magic fix. If your horse is leaning, heavy on the forehand or doesn't understand how to soften and bend that isn't going to suddenly go away. So it's as much about educating your horse, and often times the rider as well, as it is about using a different bridle.

Start groundwork before you change to riding bitless.

94.3% of those surveyed said riding bitless would be easier & more successful, if your horse had great groundwork skills (stop, turns, go, backup in a rope halter) BEFORE you did the switch to bitless

Walk your horse in hand in new places to build confidence in preparation for riding bitless. Can you walk 100 miles with your horse in 30 days?

87.7% of those surveyed said riding bitless is likely to be easier if you had walked your horse in new places on foot, to develop communication & build their confidence in new places. So they will be less likely to get nervous, spook or bolt and you will be more confident and relaxed riding.

I would not advise anyone to consider riding bitless unless you are open to putting in extra time to improve your ground skills with your horse.

Riding bitless is not just about the tool. It's about the training, it's about how you ride, it's about the cues you use, it's about clear and easy to understand communication between you and your horse, and it's about how relaxed and happy your horse feels while you ride.

Groundwork exercises

Before they switched to bitless, 86.1% of the horse riders we surveyed said they spent time doing groundwork exercises to prepare. The most common groundwork exercises people did to prepare their horses for bitless were:

- Leading at a walk on a loose rein
- Stopping and starting on a loose rein
- Turning right and left with a loose lead rope
- Backup on a loose rein
- Moving the front 180 degrees
- Moving the hind 180 degrees

Changing your riding cues

Do you need to change how you ride, when you switch from bitted to bitless? The answer is, it depends how you ride currently. The first thing to consider is contact. Almost without exception, bitless bridles and halters are designed to give the clearest signals if the rein is relaxed and "neutral" until you need to give a cue.

Once the horse responds the rider relaxes the rein immediately, letting the horse know that they have done what was asked of them. Relaxing the rein means that the reins will not be straight, they will have a slight curve in them and the horse will only feel the weight of the rein on their nose.

Many of us have been taught to ride with quite a firm feeling in the reins, which increases when we give a cue. With most bitless options you could continue to do this, but you would be missing out on the chance to use your hands more lightly and avoid the danger of desensitising your horse to the pressure.

If you are riding with a California hackamore then you absolutely cannot ride with a constant straight-rein contact. If you do you will not only desensitise your horse to the very subtle signals that are possible with a hackamore, but you will also be likely to cause them some discomfort and possibly rub the hair off of their nose.

The second thing to consider is how soft and responsive your horse is currently when you ride with a bit. If your horse currently leans on your hands or ignores your aids in a bitted bridle then the chances are that they will do the same when you ditch the bit. However, going bitless gives you a great opportunity to make a fresh start with a piece of equipment that is new to your horse. Starting with groundwork using your bitless bridle you can start working on softness and responsiveness from day one and then when you feel it's coming right, start to apply that in the saddle. If you are clear, patient and consistent you might be surprised at how different your horse can feel.

Types of bitless bridles - Rope halter

Rope halters are very popular with bitless riders. They are simple, knotted halters that can be used with the lead rope knotted to make reins, with clip on reins, or with a longer rope tied as a mecate so that there is enough to use as a lead rope while the reins are tied. There are some designs available that are made of leather.

The fit of rope halters varies widely and in some cases is pretty bad. My recommendation for a halter is that it should be well fitted. Rope halters aren't the most precise tool to ride in as they can move around quite a lot, but if they are properly fitted the aids will make more sense to your horse.

The throat piece should sit behind the horse's cheek, rather than on it. The nose band should sit comfortably above the end of the nasal bone. The nose band should also fit quite closely under the jaw without restricting how the horse moves their mouth. Long, baggy nosebands and fiador knots will affect the action of the halter, so that it acts on the horse's neck rather than its nose. They also increase the danger of your horse getting caught up on something.

When selecting the rope you might consider using a rope without a clip, so that the clip isn't swinging around when you are going above a walk.

Make sure that you know how to tie the halter up when you put it on, many come with instructions, but you can also look at on-line videos. If you tie the halter incorrectly the knot can over-tighten and be difficult to undo. Also look at how long the "tail" of the rope is after you have tied it on. If it is long enough to swing into your horse's eye either shorten it or make sure it is tucked out of the way under the cheek piece.

There is an important safety consideration when you use a rope halter, and that is that they will not break. This could be an argument for using clip-on reins that will break at the clip if your horse gets their reins caught up.

It's certainly a good reason to make sure that the halter fits properly, so that a horse that manages to sneak an itch of its head doesn't run the risk of catching a hoof or shoe in the halter. When you're riding in a rope halter, never let your horse put their head down so that it could get a front hoof caught in the reins. If you use a mecate length rope, consider what you do with it and how long the loop is when you're in the saddle. There is a reason why many horse people carry a sharp knife when they are around their horses.

Some rope halters have rings attached by the knots at the side of the noseband where you can attach reins. Similarly, it's possible to attach reins to the sides of most headcollars. If you do that then you will be riding using a sidepull action.

We recommend that you use a reputable maker when purchasing a rope halter. Some of the cheap alternatives are made of poor quality rope and fit badly. Look at photos of the halters on offer and compare them to the advice here.

Pros of rope halters:

- Instant release
- Doesn't tighten on your horse's face
- Useful also for groundwork

Cons of rope halters:

- Lacks stability on the horse's face so signals can be inconsistent
- The need to be aware that no part of the halter or rope has a break point

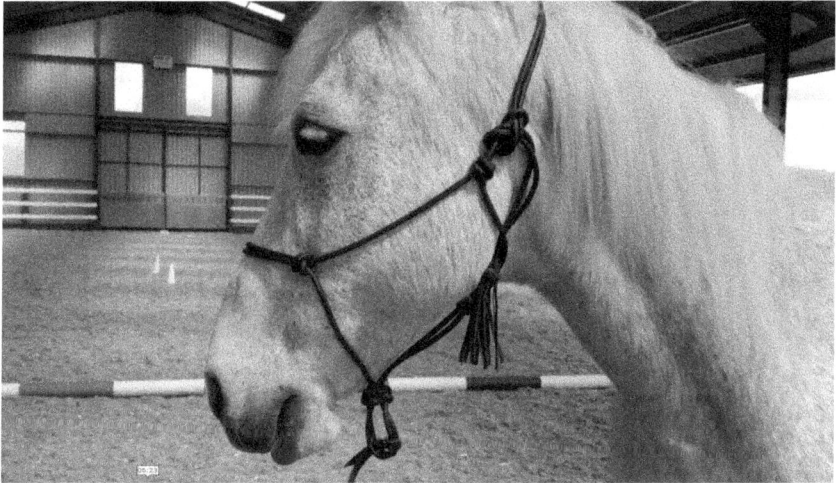

This is Ozzie my Connemara wearing a leather halter

Types of bitless bridles - Sidepull

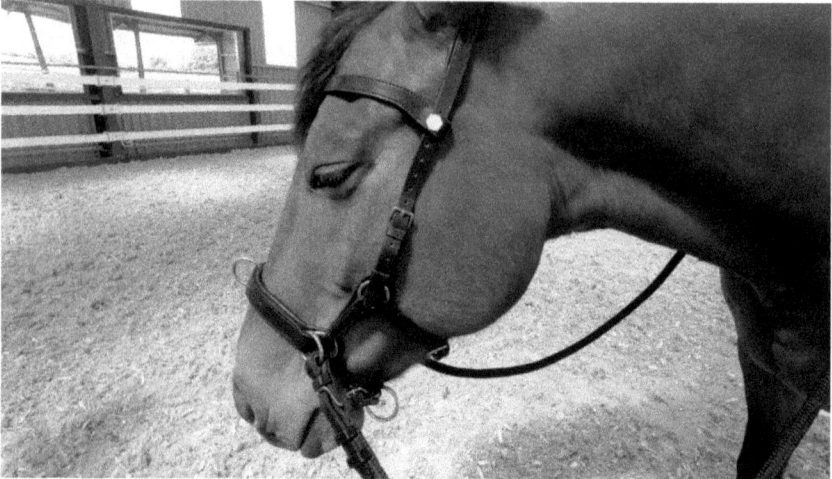

The sidepull bridle is a very simple version of a bitless bridle. Often it looks rather like a conventional bridle, but without the attachment for a bit. Your reins are attached at the side of the noseband and therefore give a very clear signal to your horse of the direction in which you want them to turn their head.

There will be a very slight pressure on the opposite side of their face from the noseband. There are a lot of unbranded sidepulls available, often from western tack suppliers. Branded options are also available. There are also some light and simple cavesson bridles that are designed to be used for riding as well as groundwork too.

Some sidepull bridles have two additional rings fitted lower down on the noseband that allow the rider to attach a second set of reins. This would give you some poll pressure and could be described as the bitless equivalent of a double bridle.

Pros of a sidepull:

- Instant release
- Doesn't use poll pressure
- Doesn't tighten on your horse's face
- Voted the second best type of bitless bridle to use for advanced riding goals by the Listening to the Horse community.

Cons of a sidepull:

- Some designs can either move on the horse's face or be quite tight
- Not used much for groundwork (unless it is a cavesson style)
- Cavessons with a metal core should be avoided as they can be harsh.

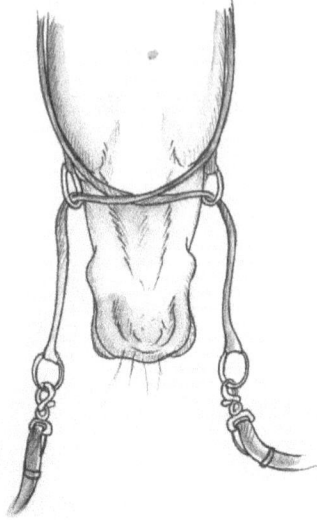

Types of bitless bridles - Cross-under and cross-over

There are two main styles of cross-under bridle. The basic cross-under will either have an extended noseband or a noseband that ends on the side of the horse's face with two straps attached to lengthen it. These straps then cross under your horse's jaw and attach to the reins. This means that cross-under bridles give your horse a different feeling to a sidepull in that they close on the jaw, the direction of feel comes more from underneath the jaw, and your horse will feel some side pressure from the noseband.

The second style of cross-under has an extended head and cheek piece that passes through rings on the noseband, crosses under your horse's jaw and attaches to the reins. So this style adds poll pressure to the action of the basic cross-under. There are some bridles that have reins attached to a strap or rope that goes over the horse's nose. These add some pressure over the nose to the sidepull action.

When you are considering any cross-under or cross-over bridle it's worth taking into account the fact that a horse's reactions to anything that closes on their head can vary.

Most horses seem to do fine with these bridles, and they are widely used successfully, just be aware that all horses are different. Also look carefully at how the straps run through the rings when you take up the rein, and check that they release instantly as soon as you give with your fingers.

Apart from considering the comfort of your horse, it would be hard to have clear signals if the cross under action was sticky.

Pros of a cross under and cross over:

- Some designs are liked because they look very similar to bitted bridles.
- Those designs that have an instant release give clear signals.

Cons of a cross under and cross over:

- Some don't release instantly.
- Because of the closing action, it is not suitable for groundwork.
- Some horses do not like the poll pressure.
- Tightens on your horse's face.

Types of bitless bridles - Hackamore (Jacuima)

Now I want to discuss what many may know as a western hackamore. This is a bosal and mecate. It is a bosal noseband with a hanger that holds it in position and a mecate tied on to make reins.

After much study I have formed the view that there is really only one style of hackamore that I like to ride with, and that is the California hackamore. So that is the style that will be discussed here.

A bosal should always have a rawhide core, it should be flexible and it should feel smooth so that it won't rub the horse's hair. This will mean that you can see a large number of strands in the surface plaiting. Normally a horse's first bosal would be a 5/8" bosal and as their education progresses they can get thinner.

When you attach the mecate to ride it becomes a hackamore. When used with a bridle, as "Two rein" then it is simply referred to as a bosal. Treasure your bosal! It should never be hung in your tack room by the hanger because the shape will become distorted. Remove the mecate after every ride to prevent that happening and coil it up to avoid it getting twisted.

The bosal should fit as snugly to your horse's face as you can manage. It should sit above the end of the nasal bone and come to rest under the chin. When the mecate is correctly wrapped you shouldn't be able to get more than two fingers in the gap between the bosal and the horse's head. The bosal should not be loose and moving around on your horse's face. This is one common mistake that is easy to notice with many riders.

Take time to shape it correctly for your horse. This may involve mysterious binding with string and maybe careful positioning of a can of beans...

Why such precision you might ask? Because a properly adjusted bosal affects the entire face. This is completely different to the action of a snaffle bit for example and that means that we have to ride differently when we use one.

If you pick up on your right rein the bosal will push on the left side of the face, for example. The bosal works on the horse's nose, meaning that you can use light vibration through your fingers to soften the poll. If your bosal is too big you lose the refinement. If it rubs your horse's head you are doing something wrong. You can't be riding with constant weight in your hands in a bosal, it's a tool that requires precise pressure and a real release.

The mecate rein is traditionally made of horsehair, but can be made of a variety of other materials including paracord, alpaca fibres and soft rope, and they come in many different colours.

Some riders find that the horsehair mecates feel prickly in their hands, but they do smooth out with wear. The average length of a mecate is 22ft but they can be up to 30ft long. Because you tie the mecate each time you ride you can vary the rein length to suit you and your horse. The spare mecate can be used for groundwork and leading. It can be secured in a variety of ways when you are in the saddle, including tucked in your belt or wrapped around a saddle horn.

Some will argue that a hackamore is "one size fits all" because it can be made to fit almost all horses by varying the number of wraps on the bosal and that you can never have too many wraps, I politely disagree. Normally there are two, possibly 3 wraps, more than that will make the bosal heavy and interfere with its refined action.

Others like the bosal to be rigid, heavier and some like it to bounce under the horse's chin when loping. I politely disagree with that as well, how uncomfortable will that be for the horse? If you can see masses of daylight around a bosal then it will move about enough to cause discomfort to your horse.

When you buy a bosal use a reputable seller who can advise you on fit and other choices. Ideally a made to measure bosal is best. Consider buying a hanger that has a tie back to keep the strap away from your horse's eye. Be wary of people selling cheap bosals and the gear to go with them on-line, the good ones aren't cheap. However they will be kind to your horse and if looked after they will last a lifetime. So be wary of buying bosals at large horse shows. I have seen very expensive bosals on sale in western stores that are made with very cheap materials, are not designed properly and would not work on any horse.

Pros:

- Instant release
- Doesn't tighten on your horse's face
- Used also in groundwork
- Voted the best type of bitless bridle to use for advanced riding goals by the Listening to the Horse community.

Cons:

- Riders need to be prepared to learn the correct riding style
- Expensive to get a properly made one as they are handmade

- Cheap ones are useless and will cause discomfort to the horse
- Not suitable for riding with a constant contact
- Easy to buy a bad one and lose money if the seller has not come personally recommended by someone with knowledge of riding in a bosal and in the California Vaquero tradition.

Types of bitless bridles - Mechanical hackamore

It's worth mentioning the other style of hackamore, which could be termed to be the mechanical hackamore. These hackamores involve some sort of metal attachment to the bridle and reins.

There are some simple mechanical hackamore options that are popular with bitless riders. An example of these would be the Flower Hackamore. This is circular with holes that allow the rider to adjust the position of the rein to exert more or less pressure on the nose and poll. Some Flower Hackamores have a short shank formed by two holes attached to the metal circle, which would allow you to have an option with stronger poll pressure.

However you would need to make the decision if you are comfortable using poll pressure on your horse. Many are not. If you have taught your horse to lower his head to put on the bridle, by touching his poll area, then this style of bitless bridle could confuse him.

Styles such as the English and German hackamores which involve longer shanks are quite a strong tool and are often used by riders who feel that they don't have enough control in a bit. I don't propose to discuss them here.

Bitless bridle problems to avoid

It is also useful to understand the most common problems that can occur when using a bitless bridle. There is no black and white with this because all people and horses are individuals, what works for one may be a problem for another, but it's useful to be aware of potential drawbacks. These are some of the issues that the survey group highlighted:

- There is no release
- There is a low release
- There is a lack of release
- The bridle has a sticky release and my horse is confused (cross over/under).
- The bridle is not gentle and is restrictive, and puts too much pressure on (cross over with constant contact).
- Some riders find with either a rope halter or a side pull, that it can move on their horse's face, may lead to sloppy communication, are not that not refined, and can lack precision.

"I have a leather bridle that was designed to work with pressure, it has two straps crossed under the chin that you connect the reins to, but they didn't release very well after application."

"I tried a cross under bitless bridle once and all of my horses hated it. I feel they objected to the restrictive nature of it. Over

communicated with pressure or in places they just aren't accustomed to.'

"When using a padded English side pull style (no cross under) I found it would shift a fair amount unless it was much tighter than I would prefer."

There were other issues identified that could be the result of poor fit, incorrect use or shoddy materials or design. In the case of all of the styles that some people found problems with, there were also people who really loved them, which just goes to prove that there is no one solution to suit all:

Benefits of using a rope halter

For many, riding in a rope halter is where their bitless experience starts. The rope halter is a simple tool that gives a bit more feel to the horse than a padded headcollar. Many horse trainers put their first rides in on a young horse using a rope halter, then progress to other options such as a snaffle bridle or hackamore. This is what the riders surveyed had to say about why they like riding in a rope halter:

- My horse is happier, more relaxed and calmer than with a bit.
- There is no metal and it can't hurt my horse's mouth.
- Riding with a rope halter directly relates to groundwork lessons learned when riding.
- It is easy to use, fast to tack up, good for quick rides.
- There is an instant release, my horse learns fast, there is good communication & responsiveness.
- With a rope halter it is easy for my horse to eat.
- I am a better rider, and can communicate more with my body.
- A rope halter is a more affordable option for me.
- I like that there is no bit in cold weather.

Benefits of using a hackamore

I don't mind admitting that the California Hackamore is a bit of a favourite of mine. When you relax the rein on a hackamore it will sit completely neutrally on your horse's head, which means that your release is clear. When you want to pick up and talk to your horse through the rein it is a refined tool; signals from even the tiniest movement of your little finger can be felt by your horse. With that comes a responsibility to learn to use the tool correctly so that you and your horse get most benefit from it, but that can be a very rewarding study.

The responses from the horse riders surveyed showed that they were interested in these hackamores as well. The following highlights just a small sample of their comments:

12 reasons people use a bosal & mecate

Here are some case studies from riders who are currently riding with a bosal and mecate.

1. The horse doesn't fight anymore, avoids pain, and the horse is more relaxed and happier than in a bit.

"I found my horse was more comfortable and he didn't fight the hackamore like he did the bit. He is just as responsive in the hackamore and has better concentration as he is not worrying/fighting the bit."

"My mare is 23 and has never really liked a bit in her mouth. I have tried several styles of bitless bridles with no so much success as she clearly was not all that happy. Approximately six months ago I started using the California Hackamore and we haven't looked back. She is calm, willing and her whole attitude and carriage has softened'.

'My horse is more relaxed in his hackamore than in his snaffle. He offers a softer feel back through the reins. I did have a custom one made for him."

"My mare is much more relaxed in the hackamore. She has a low palate and a shallow mouth. I just couldn't find a bit that she was comfortable in, so she was always stiff and resistant. She is a different horse in the hackamore!"

"I introduced my mare to this about 3 months ago, with encouragement from a friend and trainer. She is much happier, much less anxious than she ever was with a bit. (I used to ride in a French-link snaffle, as this girl has a low palate.) She now puts her nose willingly in the bosal - something that NEVER happened with a bit and bridle. We're working on relaxation, since this mare is a tense, fizzy little horse. It's helping and she's realizing that she doesn't have to do things fast to get them over with."

2. You ride skills improve a lot when you use a hackamore, compared to a halter or bit

"With my hackamore I have learnt to have really good listening hands. It has helped me refine my cues and signals and has allowed me to refine my riding to one hand, using the smallest signals. I am not familiar with other forms of bitless bridle. I do not see the appeal. I doubt that they can match the hackamore for refinement. I am of course prepared to be enlightened!"

"'I always liked the refinement of the hackamore as well as the fact that to have a good hackamore horse you need to be more in tune and get into your horses mind and get them to want to do as you ask - instead of making them do what you want."

"Riding with a hackamore raises my level of awareness of: how position, location, feel, & signal of my: hands, body language, rein position can influence the communication to the horse."

"Riding with a hackamore has helped me learn to not hold a steady pull on my horse. My release has become better, and my horse has gotten softer as a result."

"'The subtle signalling you use with a hackamore encourages light hands."

"'I have just got my first California hackamore and like it because it is so precise with its signals and I can ride with a soft contact."

"Riding with a hackamore enables me to use clear and simple cues that can get even softer."

3. The horse is more calm, connected and has more confidence when ridden in a hackamore

"I like riding with a hackamore t because the horse is calm and we have a better connection."

"My horse is more confident when she wears a hackamore when cutting cattle."

"My horse seems more comfortable and relaxed and is actually more responsive than when using a bit.'"

4. The hackamore is more precise, and is easier to understand for the horse, compared to a rope halter

"Direct application of aids (which are a lot better than when riding with rope halter., My horse is a lot more responsive when riding with a hackamore. He gives better to the reins, and he bends better."

"I feel like I can give more clearly understood cues with this equipment."

"The bosal allows me to refine my horsemanship skills. The rope halter allows me to teach my horse the basics of ridden lightness."

"You can give your horse lots of signal before you pick up contact. You can't force anything so you have to be better at feeling for your horse and waiting for him to find the answer. Also, all three of our horses seem to prefer a traditional hackamore (bosal and mecate) to a bit."

"Riding with a hackamore makes my hands have better feel with the horse, to be lighter, and my horse is lighter."

5. The horse is lighter and more responsive

"When I do ride in a hackamore my horse is so much lighter and more responsive than in a bitless bridle."

"The responsiveness I get without any mouth harm is wonderful"

"I didn't like it at first after moving from utilizing a snaffle for 30+ years. After getting used to signals, I love how light my horse has become in using it. It's a joy to use. He was started in a 5/8" bosal and has been in a 1/4" bosalita for 4 years."

6. They like the tradition and to use a piece of art while they ride

"Love the look and tradition; when well made, excellent balance."

"I like the tradition and that the good ones are functional art."

7. You don't need to deal with a cold bit during the winter

"I ride my present horses both bitted and bitless, depending on the weather (I don't like to use cold bits in winter) and what I am doing."

8. You can compete in western dressage

"My horse enjoys it! He is soft, relaxed, more supple in all directions. Also there is no bit to warm up in the winter. I can compete in western dressage with it as well."

9. It uses a quick release of pressure

"Riding with a hackamore allows me a quick release of pressure."

"It's simplicity and it has a good release."

10. It is good for beginners as you won't hurt your horse's mouth.

"I like that I am not worrying about hurting my horse's mouth while I gain skills."

11. When you are on a long ride it is easier for your horse to drink & snack

"I like how my horse responds to the hackamore and for long rides it makes it much easier for him to drink and grab snacks along the way as I like to make sure he always has food in his GI tract."

12. You can lead a horse and do groundwork with the get down rope

"I like the extra lead rope for leading/ground work. It is lightweight and doesn't require a cold bit in the winter. If you know how to tie a mecate knot, it pretty much fits any horse. (It also fits my cow!)."

"There is no bit, and it has a built in lead line. This makes it very helpful for trails going through gates."

Should you try riding bitless?

I asked our equestrian community what advice they would give to anyone who is interested in trying out bitless. They had a lot of advice to give. Here is a selection of their thoughts.

Give it a try.

"Go for it! Your horse will thank you. And remember you still need light hands and to pay attention to what your horse thinks and feels."

"Don't be afraid to try, go slow and see how your horse responds. If you don't feel comfortable you can always go back to the bit."

"Do it!! (But pay attention to the fit. I tried 3 different bitless bridles before I found the one that my horse responded best to)."

"Try to do as much research as possible and experiment with which type of bridle is best for your horse, always ensuring a good fit. When you come to buy your bridle, invest in the most well made you can and look after it. Always put the horse first and don't be afraid to change or adjust bridles to find where your horse is happy."

Do your research.

"Just try it! Start slow, do your research on how each bitless bridle works and find something quality."

"Maybe try and borrow a bitless bridle from someone to see if it suits your horse as they have many different styles. Really it's the way to go. I think a bitless bridle suits all horses it's suiting the rider. Some people would not feel secure and that raises a whole lot of questions about the rider and their approach to horsemanship."

Choose a bitless bridle with clear & instant release

"Get and use a bitless bridle that provides a clear and distinct release of pressure. Do a lot of groundwork to ensure that your horse fully understands and is practiced with the bitless bridle."

Begin safely

"If you are worried just start in a small yard where things can't get out of hand."

"When you are comfortable with groundwork, they're light and calm, try it. Get on just walk a circle in a place they are comfortable and have a friend to be ground support."

"Practice in a ring and area close to home till you and horse are comfortable"

Go slowly

"Listen to your horse and take your time. If you already have light hands with a bit, the transition should be simple. Don't be afraid to try, just allow time to introduce at your horse's pace."

When using bitless - Consider the need to change how you ride

"Just do it. The horse understands pretty fast. The main thing is to have soft hands so that you don't "wear out the brakes". Lots of English style riders feel the need to have contact at all times and never let their horse have a nice loopy rein. They are terrified that the horse will take off if they release any tension. This type of rider will have trouble surrendering to the trust required and will have issues with bitless. (The horse will have no problem as the brakes are in the head)."

"How much do you rely on your bit right now? Can you direct your horse, including a stop, without much contact in the reins? Will your horse understand the new steering method? Then go ahead and switch. Otherwise work on that first."

"Practice using leg and seat cues before using the reins/bit. If the horse doesn't get what you're asking, then immediately reinforce with reins/bit. My experience with my horse is that after practicing this way for a while, he no longer needs hand cues. This is such a

fantastic feeling and seems as though we are really connected. It is as though I only have to think about what we want to do and he does it! Amazing!"

"Understand that not all pressure is the same and it is the release of pressure that is the major cue."

"If the horse is happy in a bit and your connection with the mouth is soft and more about the sharing of information, rather than a control device, ask yourself why you need to change. If you decide to change, remember that unless you're using a soft wide side pull bridle, you can still hurt your horse with hard hands. It's not about bits or bitless, it's about how you use your hands and your communication with your horse... you have to be willing to listen to the feedback and suggestions as well as you are at making them."

"I think a lot of people might shy away from bitless because they may feel it gives them less control. I feel that if that might be the case, perhaps they should go back to basics to really get the horse responding to their aids, including voice and pressure and release, to ensure that their horse can respond to pressure from a bitless bridle. My 17'2 warm blood was never very good with slowing down. It's still something we're working on but I found he was much better in a bitless bridle than a bit. After all, shouldn't we be working on having a good partnership with our horses rather than a dictatorship?"

Prepare with groundwork

"If your horse follows a feel on the halter well, it will probably work fine in a bitless bridle."

"Do plenty of groundwork and don't rush it."

"Do the groundwork in a rope halter first."

"Learn to use your body correctly, using energy and intention for ground work, which then carries over to riding."

"Teach your horse everything new from the ground until he knows what you want before trying it from the saddle."

"Know your horse. What does your horse already know? Teach start, stop, back up, turn both ways, lateral flexion on the ground first in halter. Then with a rider, teach hindquarter yield and emergency stop. Then go for it."

"Groundwork and walking your horse on foot is important whether you ride with or without a bit. Your horse should and can respond equally well without a bit. A bit will not stop a fearful or excited horse."

"Check out your horse's responses to the bitless gear on the ground first, do you have flexion and relaxation? When starting to ride, begin in a yard or arena and make sure your horse is relaxed and

accepting of gear before advancing the environment and or movement."

"Definitely do loads of groundwork and get that really good and soft before you transition to bitless. Your horse should be able to follow a feel and know what subtle cues are about and be able to move their body in response to a cue. The rider has to be consistent and unambiguous with light hands. I think there has to be really good lines of communication between horse and rider before you start."

Get TrailBrave

"I think two things are important one - you cannot underestimate the impact and development of your relationship with your horse by spending undemanding time with them as well as what Steve Halfpenny talks about in his Trail Brave program. Two - get a solid foundation and communication on the ground first with lightness and understanding, asking and establishing all the communication that you would ask and expect while riding. Achieve lightness there first."

Buy only good quality and make sure it fits

"Make sure it fits properly and is good quality and do get the horse used to it by walking in it and giving to pressure in all directions."

"Do not buy a cheap California hackamore."

"Do not buy a poor quality bitless bridle."

How to begin riding bitless

"You need good groundwork, softness/lightness and confidence. Just because there's no bit, doesn't mean you get to manhandle the reins either."

"Make sure that the horse understands from the ground what you may ask of them and both horse and rider know how to do an emergency stop! Just in case..."

"Do groundwork exercises first, and ride in an arena or safe paddock before you venture out, and make sure you have a good stop established. Make sure you know how to disengage the hindquarters and can implement a one rein stop if you need to. If you struggle with bitless, then there is likely a gap in your training, it's not that your horse 'can't do bitless'. Teach your horse to stop on your breath, and use your body, not your hands. There is far too much reliance on hands. It's easier to ride with a bit in most cases; so you will need to take the time to build a relationship with your horse, rather than seeking to 'control' your horse by pulling at a hunk of metal in their mouth. It's ultimately so worth it."

"Ensure basic groundwork (as ticked above) is good. Ensure lateral flexion is working well. If possible, start in a round pen. Don't overthink it. Your horse already knows how to move off pressure. Have fun!"

"Try it in an arena or paddock and with a friend or coach present. My first try was very positive."

Try to borrow a California hackamore (if it suits you, it is the most subtle and refined bitless tool to enable you to improve your riding skills).

"My opinion is that California style hackamore gives the most consistent signal. Get or borrow a good one & see what your horse tells you about it. Try other bitless options if your horse doesn't like it…"

"Try it in a lesson or clinic so you can get help if you need it. Your horse will let you know if he likes a California Hackamore or not. Mine sure did!

"I prefer the way a horse looks (softer more relaxed) when in collection with the California hackamore."

"Definitely give it a go. I was the biggest sceptic when I first saw Steve Halfpenny ride in a California hackamore (bosal & mecate). I remember saying, "you'll never see me ride with one of those things'. Now it's what I ride in most. Just like all things, get your horse used to it and work on the ground with one to make sure your horse understands the signals. Above all things, keep your hands soft and as Steve says, "do anything but pull"."

If you are interested in riding with a California hackamore:

"You should look for a Bosal made by a good braider, that fits your horse. Don't take a cheap one from a "discounter". When you buy cheap than you buy twice. Quality bosal & mecates start at $350 to $400 upwards."

"You should only buy from a highly recommended bosal maker. 99.9% of hackamores seen at trade shows (both cheap and expensive) are of poor quality and not suitable to use on a horse. At Equitana in 2018 there were a few shops selling hackamore, some expensive (500 to 600 euros!), all of poor quality."

"Cheap hackamores are not made properly, have incorrect materials, are often rough to touch and will not work for you and your horse. Don't waste your money.

"Read the book The California Hackamore Horse by Jeff Sanders. Take the time to get the right Hackamore and fit it properly to your horse. Make sure you have the proper ground work done prior to starting the Hackamore."

"Do your groundwork first, getting your horse used to the feel of the California Hackamore. Talk to your horse. Tell him that you would like to try this because you think it will be kinder to him. Then when you ride, remember, light hands. You should be using mostly your legs, seat bones and slight shifts of weight."

"Go for it, but make sure you fit the hackamore, it doesn't work well when it is placed wrong, or doesn't fit."

Rope halter success stories

The rope halter is a very popular tool for bitless riding. For some it's the place where they start before moving on to other options such as the hackamore. For others it's the tool that they think works best for them and their horse and they look no further. Here are just some of the success stories shared in the survey:

"I rode a lot in a rope halter or hackamore and enjoyed using this equipment and my fell pony went well in it. Even the more collected type riding was ok. All our riding was done this way. I liked the lightness of the equipment and the speed of response and the feeling of the rope reins."

"When my now 20 year old competition horse was 3, he lost a tooth which got stuck in the chin and created some pain. The vet told me to continue with starting him under saddle but skip the bit for four weeks. I didn't have anything else than a rope halter at the time. And it turned out to work just fine."

"I use a rope halter because it's quick and easy to use. I can transition from my ground work to riding without changing equipment out. I tend to use a rope halter first and transition to a bitless bridle when training a horse. I feel I have more "control" in a rope halter just in case something happens where I need to bend quickly to a stop. I also love that it's lightweight and loose around the nose so the horse can feel free and unrestricted moving forwards."

"I use a rope halter. My horse is very forward and throws his head with a bit. He is a Tennessee Walker and was a show horse thus has a lot of the nervous habits that show horses can develop. When I took the bit away, we started communicating more like we do with groundwork and he was less preoccupied with the bit. I am not formally trained to ride but I have self-educated in natural horsemanship. For my purposes, our communication is better without the distraction of a bit. I don't really understand how they work, so I wouldn't want to give conflicting cues. My horse is gaited, and I enjoy his natural gait and don't care to use a bit to force an unnatural one."

"I ride with a rope halter but hope to get a California hackamore eventually. I prefer this for my horse as he is sensitive and is remarkably calmer when bitless, and therefore more tuned in to what I am asking of him, and less likely to get upset when things don't go well."

"What I like best about using a rope halter, is that it's taught me how responsive a horse is to cues that have nothing to do with a bit, and how to communicate with my horse with my body."

"I ride in rope halters because I can make them to fit my horses well, they are inexpensive and my horses respond well to them. I like being able to hop off my horse and lead them or walk them if I need to. I used to have horses that would toss their heads or grab the bit, would buck or throw fits and I just don't see the same behaviors with my halters, and if I do it seems very manageable with a little education to the horse. I've gotten several "problem horses" and when removing the bit and starting over with halter educating things progress very quickly and when I go back to the bit they seem very obstinate and unhappy, so I just stay with the halter. I haven't had any issues on trails or at shows with my halter yet."

"We typically ride with a rope halter attached to a 12' lead under our bridles. Gives you a way to work through potential issues from the ground and is a good insurance policy should the need to walk home or trail tie."

"I like that doesn't hurt his mouth. It forces me to become better with my leg cues and balance. I think it has greatly improved our relationship. He trusts me not to hurt him and is more willing to try."

"I ride with a rope halter on the trail for numerous reasons. First, it is easier on the horse and requires a closer relationship with him/her. As a rider I use my legs more and leave my horses face pretty much alone. I don't need to change from a headstall to a halter if I get off the horse. I save the bit for more refined work in the arena. Even in the arena, I use a halter a lot of the time to encourage communication with my body and his."

"I originally switched to bitless (actually a headcollar and lead rope initially) for my Arab mare who was very forward and who fought any and every bit I tried, all of which were mild. She and I never looked back, she took to it like a duck to water and we never had any serious disagreement about speed after that."

"Going bitless isn't for everyone or every horse.........but it has certainly helped my horse as he had significant wear on his teeth when I bought him, due to chomping down on a bit!"

"After having bought an ex camp-drafter who was being ridden in a twisted snaffle because he 'wouldn't stop' I now ride him bitless on the halter setting and he stops on a long, light rein. There is no need to have a bit in his mouth. He neck reins and stops on voice command. It's interesting to me that he was ever hard to stop. I see no need for bits if you train your horse correctly to be ridden bitless".

"I was a horse science major in college, and we always started youngsters riding with just a halter on, because you want to stay out of their mouth while they are adjusting to carrying your weight."

Bitless bridle success stories

The survey group also had a lot to say about their successes with bitless bridles. Again, too many to include all of them, so here is just a sample. They are encouraging reading for anyone who is considering taking the plunge to bitless.

Starting horses.

"I would have to say starting a horse bitless I have experienced a mutual feeling of lightness. Even though my Gypsy is a heavy girl she is the lightest horse I've ever known. I have had her since she was 5 months old and always felt a connection. I'm glad we carried the connection on when backing her with the bitless bridle. My off the track Thoroughbred became a different softer happier horse when I restarted him bitless."

I worry less!

"I know that some people say a bitless bridle is for training a young horse but I find I learned so much from using a side pull. Due to a health condition my horse was going through we had to switch to a side pull if we wanted to continue to ride. I was worried. The first ride sold me on it. My horse was much more relaxed and the riding balance and use of leg cues I learned is priceless. The art of hand

stillness is well worth the price of the tack and the nerves. Now I worry when I use a bit. Imagine that!"

I can be more gentle.

"We made up a bitless bridle and we love it so far. Our horse is nearly 5 and only been sat on and tacked up. We tried getting him to accept a bit which he does but we don't feel that a generic bit will fit any horses' mouth and anyway why use a bit if your ground work has been so good that you only have to whistle, click and say wait. We feel that the gentler you are the more you will get out of your horse. Our loan pony is ridden in a snaffle bit but my daughter rides her more often in a head collar and bare back, she is much better behaved when we do this."

Increased calmness and relaxation and better on trail rides.

"I chose a bitless bridle because my horse always seemed on edge and wanted to go jig jog all day. I tried lots of this to bring her down. I researched bitless bridles, gave one a go, and wow I had a different horse. So calm, much more relaxed, never looked back."

"As a fairly new rider, I feel it is teaching me to rely less on my hands and more on my legs and seat. Plus it gives me the confidence that I am not hurting the horse's mouth. I started using a sidepull after the horse had some mouth issues and discovered my hands can be quiet and the horse seemed more relaxed."

"I drive my pony with a bitless bridle. She loves it and can't wait to put it on. She hates a bit in her mouth and is very tense if I use it. Bonnie is very obliging with her bitless bridle."

"My pony would not open her mouth for her (very mild) bit. I tried a bitless bridle and she instantly was happy about being bridled. I then got a horse who was very forward and stressed. I replaced her martingale and bitted bridle to bitless, and she literally sighed and relaxed instantly. Have you ever put a piece of metal in your mouth such as the handle of a spoon? See what it does to your salivary glands. How can a horse fully engage its attention on its rider when its digestive system is being stimulated in such a big way?"

"I ride in a bitless bridle, and have ridden this way for the past 12 years. It was essential in rehabilitating my Percheron cross rescue who was so very untrusting of humans. With my QH she is so much happier and more willing. She often asks to go for a ride. It has made a huge difference in building strong mutually respectful relationships. I am so glad the momentum is building and the popularity has grown so that more horses can benefit from the use of bitless riding."

"Since changing from a lifelong mild curb bit, my 22 yr old gelding, formerly very hot and anxious on the trail who would NEVER walk, has relaxed so much more, stretches out his neck, and we can both just enjoy the ride. Yes we are still retraining, as old habits die hard...but he will never have a bit in his mouth again - there is simply no need. For those who are afraid to lose control of their

horse, the key is practicing and knowing that you have hind end disengagement whenever you need it."

"My son has a bitless bridle made by a fellow endurance rider. My son had a fairly excitable Arab and this bridle worked beautifully with her. He was able to use a very gentle hand and get great results. She responded so well to it. When we first got her, she would spook at the oddest times and at the oddest things (like a truck and trailer that had been parked by her paddock for a couple weeks). This bridle was ideal because it still made my son use a gentle approach when it can be easy to over react. Soon, his mare had settled much more and he was able to take her on the trails with no concern."

"I love riding bitless and my horses love it too. I will never use a bit again on any of my 4 horses. I ride my ex-racehorse bitless and he is so much more relaxed and happy. All were easy to train to bitless."

"I have a youngster that will also go into a bitless bridle once he's started. I believe that my horses prefer to be without that solid piece of steel in their mouths. They just seem happier and are more relaxed, especially relaxed in their mouths."

"Horse will be less spooky without a bit in their mouth. Mine were. They also relaxed more and were not bracy in the front end. The big issue I have run up against with my friends is that they all still believe you can't stop or control a horse without a bit. Therefore, they can't relax in the saddle without a bit in the horse's mouth. I can tell you from first-hand experience, if a horse is going to bolt, buck, or spin - it does not matter what they have in their mouth and it is your skill in gaining control that is going to matter. The horse will also come under control easier without the pain of bit pressure in their mouth."

Easier to put the bridle on.

"My horses love the bitless bridle. They are more relaxed and responsive with lighter hands, and now that they know the difference, they don't fuss when I go to put the bridle on. They're just happier without the metal in their mouths, especially my Paso whose former owners rode her in a Paso bit. She no longer sends her nose high in the air and clamping her teeth when I start putting her bridle on."

The horse doesn't pull or root any more.

"First off my horse loves it. He was given to me and had several issues I had to work through. The first was he would root with a bit, so I never rode him with a bridle, I started with my bitless. He never pulled on it and loved it. I know I wasn't the best with my hands and didn't want to cause more of a problem. Using the bitless made me use my seat more and my hands less, I have been riding bitless for over 25 years now."

My horse fusses less without a bit.

"I ride in a western style side pull bitless. Ever since being started as a 5 year old, I have had bitting issues with my Paint gelding, trying a seemingly endless array of bits on him. He was always mouthy and pulled weird faces when ever worked. Eventually I tried a bitless on him and we both loved it. He is responsive and soft as never before."

"I have been listening to lots of so-called authorities on this subject for many years pros and cons of the debate. In the end my horse told me the answer, if I have the bridle with the bit he clams his mouth shut and puts his head away and up. The bitless he pushes his face into it so I guess that is answer enough."

My horse has stopped bolting.

"I use a side pull type with my OTT standardbred. He really resented having a bit in his mouth, something to do with his racing days I'm sure. I tried several bits and had issues with bolting, he would brace against any lateral pressure and constantly playing with the bit and putting his tongue over it. Since trying bitless he's an absolute pleasure to ride, almost as soft as my quarter horse."

My horse stopped rearing up.

"Indi, a TB came 20+ years ago with a rearing and bucking habit ... I discovered that this was because she was incredibly sensitive, and simply responded to the slightest mouth or poll pressure by going up in the air. After a nasty fall, I started riding her in her halter. It was a huge turning point for us both. I eventually went on to a side pull, and went on to enjoy many years with her before retiring her 3 years ago."

"With my first horse, I was using a simple low curb fixed shank western bit. I was confident and was constantly told that I had light hands, rode with loose rein, western, no problem. A lot of the riding was trail or suburban streets. She had a rearing habit. I switched to a hackamore (bosal and mecate) and the rearing stopped, her head became relaxed and she was much happier."

Less likely to hurt the horse when showjumping

"I used to be afraid to ride my horse with the bitless because I did not trust how much control I would have. I like to jump my horse and sometimes if I am behind her I can hit her in the mouth and with the bitless I will not hurt her mouth. She is better on the trails because with the bit she would sometimes grab it and take off. With the bitless she cannot do that. I find she is happier with the bitless. I hope soon that most horse shows will accept the bitless in their rules on tack attire."

It fixed my horse's head tossing and head shaking issues.

"I love it because my horse is so much happier in it. She's a Dutch warm blood event horse, but we ride out in the California hills mostly jumping logs and galloping over hills. She puts her head right into her bit less bridle, while getting her to take the bit was a constant struggle. She would toss her head constantly while on the trail with a bit, and is so much quieter now. We tried every kind of bit and tooth issue before I got her this beautiful bitless bridle from Portugal. I just love it."

"I now own a little mare who is 10yrs old and trained to ride, but has not had much time under saddle and would prefer to not work much. She seemed to dislike the mild snaffle, so I started using the side pull. Much less protesting and head shaking. I am training her to respond to leg, seat, body and mind aids and trying to be very minimal with the hands/reins, so I think going bitless is helpful to us. I also quite often just clip reins to her web halter (snugged up a bit for better contact) with good results too."

"I ride with the first bitless bridle I have ever tried which is a simple side pull. It is really simple and my horse goes so well in it - she is calm as opposed to when I got her, she was in a snaffle bit and bridle with a martingale attachment and spent all her time trying to toss her head around and fight all the paraphernalia! Now we have simplified it, she is so calm and chilled out. It's brilliant!"

My horse is more responsive without a bit.

"I have my girl in an English bridle with a bitless noseband converter attached to the bridle. I love it because my horse loves it, when she sees the bridle now she actually puts her head into it herself unlike when we had the bit she would shy away from it. She is a lot more responsive with the bitless bridle as well. I love the fact we no longer have a metal contraption in her mouth hurting her."

Riding bitless has improved my dressage and riding skills.

"I have ridden dressage for many years and had read several articles about how snaffle bits weren't as "forgiving" as I had

thought. I have to admit that I was quite sceptical of how effective a bitless bridle could be. But much to my surprise, my horse was softer, more responsive, and quieter with his head than he had been in the loose ring snaffle I had used for many years! I realize that these bitless bridles still use pressure but I do think they are easier on the horse. Any equipment used improperly or with malice can cause pain to or equine partners. So all must be used with respect."

"I have tried riding with a bitless bridle just a few times. Mostly I ride with a snaffle or rubber bit. Riding with a bitless bridle happened for the first time because my instructor wanted me to have new experience and wanted to make me communicate with a horse using a bitless bridle. It went very well, I was forced to use my body language and balance more, and I loved the experience."

"I take dressage lessons and hack around the barn property. I don't show. If I did, I would still use the bitless even though that would eliminate me from placing. What I like most of all is that I don't put a piece of metal in his mouth (although he has never been difficult to bridle with a bit), I don't have to warm the bit up in the winter and if I mistakenly tug on the reins, it doesn't pull back on his mouth."

"I have only just got my first bitless bridle. I had one on trial for a couple of weeks & was really pleased with it, my horse seemed more relaxed, stretched his neck & blew his nose in canter for the first time ever. And I like that it has an ergonomic shaped headpiece which I've found most bitless bridles haven't."

Great for novice riders.

"I am a therapeutic riding instructor and started using bitless for all my students because I hated seeing novice riders or those with learning disabilities be hard on the horse's mouth. I found that the horses are happier and that there really is no reason to put a bit in their mouth, especially when doing arena work or riding lessons. Some horses we just use a halter, but as the riders advance in their skills, the bitless bridle teaches them to use their hands properly and carry the reins correctly. It's great for all of us!"

Hackamore success stories

As I've said earlier, the California hackamore is very popular with our Listening to the Horse community around the world. Consequently they had a lot to say about how well it has worked for them. Here are some of their success stories:

Young horse training.

"I love the fact that all our horses are much happier in our hackamores. We start all the new horses in a bosal and they all respond so well. Because all the groundwork is done prior, they understand the signals from the bosal straight away. There is no pulling or inflicting unnecessary pain for them to understand. Horses

that come here with issues from bridles are put straight into bosals and all are way happier almost immediately. This gives us a chance to work on their mind and figure out what the issue has been. Generally once that is sorted, they can go back into the bit providing it is correctly fitted and their mouth allows for a bit. Personally, my good horses will stay in a bosal, unless I ever reach the stage of a bridle horse."

"I've started using a California Hackamore for both of my mares. The first I used it was for my now 4yo. They are not a popular item you see in my area, but wanted to try it. I knew Nixie had her wolf teeth, so didn't want to start her with a bit yet. I had tried leading her in the bitless I have for my gelding, but she would shake her head, and didn't like it when it would tighten around her nose. She took very well to the bosal, and this is the only thing I've ridden her in. She does beautifully with it, and I'd like to stick with it. I'll eventually introduce her to a bit, so she will understand it if anything ever happens to me and she has another home, but while with me, I'd like to keep her with the hackamore. My 20yo Arab/QH had been using other bits. She can be hot, would buck going into a canter, and wouldn't listen well with a snaffle. When I got the hackamore for the 4yo, I figured, why not give it a try? She surprised me with how well she responded to it. She didn't buck going into a canter, making me believe that her issue was the bit I had used before. I game with her (barrels, poles, etc) and haven't tried that yet with the hackamore, but I plan to give it a go this year!"

Dressage riding.

"Both my horse and I are very happy with this rig. We compete at the national level in western Dressage and have received numerous compliments & high scores on our harmony & connection which is well represented using the California Hackamore."

Rider refinement.

"With my hackamore I have learnt to have really good listening hands. It has helped me refine my cues and signals and has allowed me to refine my riding to one hand, using the smallest signals. I am not familiar with other forms of bitless bridle, however I do not see the appeal. I doubt that they can match the hackamore for refinement."

"I always liked the refinement of the hackamore as well as the fact that to have a good hackamore horse you need to be more in tune and get into your horses mind and get them to want to do as you ask instead of making them do what you want."

"I like the way my mare responds to it. I'm certain most of it is due to the fact there is no bit involved. She hates having a bit in her mouth. The hackamore allows her to focus more of what we are doing instead of the piece of metal in her mouth. I can be softer with my cues and get good responses. It's getting better all the time but i don't have any experienced hackamore instructors in our area so our progress is slower than I'd like. I also like the way it looks on her."

A calm and happy horse.

"I purchased my Hackamore in September 2019. We love it. My horse and I had a hard time finding something that fit him just right. He would start tossing his head and chewing if I asked something that was new or challenging to him. With this hackamore I have been riding with since September, I have not seen that behaviour at all. He is much more responsive to my body cues and is much smoother as well.

My mare is much more relaxed in the hackamore. She has a low palate and a shallow mouth. I just couldn't find a bit that she was comfortable in, so she was always stiff and resistant. She is a different horse in the hackamore!"

"I first tried bitless (hackamore) as I had a new horse as a 7yo (who is now 23 yo) who told me over several months that she was not happy and over time she deteriorated around the head... so in desperation I tried a hackamore for the first time in my life (and yes it was a scary thing for me)... and we went forward from that moment on! She is a big mover and a real powerhouse but respected the freedom from the bit. On trails I feel so much more comfortable for them without a bit for eating and drinking, tying up etc. Happy horses!"

It offers easy communication between horse and rider.

"I have tried many bitless bridles and inventions. The bosal hackamore has proven to me the best results. I wish an English version could be invented that has the same effect as the bosal/hackamore. In short, you can train a horse to anything they are the most adaptable creatures on the planet. I just like the road to be comfortable, with clear and comfortable, easy communication from horse to rider and vice versa. The bosal hackamore seems to do that for me."

Final thoughts

Well, it's been a lot of fun putting this book together. I hope it's been useful for you. Here are some final thoughts to consider from current bitless bridle equestrians:

Dressage competitions:

"There needs to be more push for the use of bitless bridles, especially at high level dressage the compulsory use of double bridles needs to stop."

"Currently, bits are the default and there seems to be the attitude of 'there must be a reason to choose bitless'. I would like to see it swing the other way where bitless is the default and "there must be a reason to choose to use a bit."

Ethics:

"It would be nice to be part of a world where horses are not systematically and deliberately hurt as part of the horse/rider partnership."

Bitless challenge:

"I think everyone should try riding bitless at least for a month. It improves communication through your body and teaches a rider to

be less reliant on the reins e.g. teaches mindfulness, softness of hands, use of your core, weight transference etc."

Every ride needs gentle and thoughtful hands:

"No matter what your choice is it all comes down to your hands, they need to be very soft and light and with a lot of respect for the horse."

"A bitless rider needs to be a thinking rider, light in their hands, willing to make sure there horse understands a one rein stop & lateral flexion before heading out of the round pen. Bitless is kinder to the horse because a bit in the mouth is a stress they can never solve, they just learn to accept the discomfort or shut down to it."

"I think that there are very few people who are good enough to ride with a bit and when it has been proven that everything is possible without it, why do we persist with it?"

"As lovers of horses it is always important to understand & bear in mind that there are no short cuts or gimmicks that will improve your riding experience. Time and more time with focus & purpose is the best method of furthering your understanding & relationship with all horses. No need to resort to harsher means, severe bits or bigger spurs...Light hands, clear cues, more time with realistic expectations for each individual horse will take one far toward getting the most out of each equine relationship! :-)"

Great for trail rides:

"Bitless is the way to go! My horse can eat and drink more easily on the trail!"

If your horse has head, mouth or teeth issues, try bitless as an experiment.

"My horse had all sorts of problems with bits, couldn't find anything she liked. So I just decided to stop using them. She's much happier."

A hackamore is not designed to be ridden with a constant contact.

"Riders should be aware that if they choose to ride in a hackamore, they need to understand how it works, it's not like having contact all the time in a bit."

Less gadgets, work on the relationship instead.

"Changing a "tradition" of bits, shoes, whips and spurs takes time and a willingness on the owner to learn and embrace a different way of thinking. To be brave and rely more on your relationship and feelings than just hanging on the hope of more and more paraphernalia.

"It's heart-warming to see the trend toward using less force and gadgets to communicate with our wonderful equine companions."

Don't just copy other riders you admire.

Just because some big name says to use a bit, doesn't mean you should! Study what bits do in a horse's mouth! The old Californio way is a wonderful style of horsemanship that really honors the horse and puts the horse first in every aspect. I wish more "big name" people would study the California traditions."

A snaffle is not always the best option.

"I used to use a bit and bridle (snaffle) like most people but since realising how it affects the horse I prefer the halter. People think you need a bit for control but it doesn't work that way."

The horse should enjoy his work too.

"My opinion is that if the horse doesn't like bits, you shouldn't ride them with a bit. And if that means there are things you can't do (like certain competitions where you have to have bits) so be it. The horse must have a say in what you do together, and he must be able to enjoy it too. If you are having problems with everyday riding without a bit, you just need to work more on your relationship with the horse, to get the partnership and communication that you need for it to work. I think it is our job to adjust our riding to our horses, not the other way around."

Relationships are built on the ground.

"I've transitioned at least 15 horses to bitless for my lesson program without any issues. We just start them at a walk and go through our regular halt and three emergency halts. When I grew up horses were never put under saddle with a bit in their mouth, it was always with a hackamore (bitless bridles, like we have today, were not available). The groundwork I've said I do above, is what I do with all our horses and ponies because I believe relationship are built on the ground, not from their backs, so we do a lot of things on the ground with the horses and it is all groundwork I'd do if using a bit as well. I've always felt that bits were intended to enhance communication and that they were never intended for control. I also feel that people that feel a horse needs a bit in its mouth for them to be safe to ride the horse, shouldn't be riding. They should be doing more groundwork with their horse and learn better use of their breathing, seat and legs."

"You can't do too much ground work."

Finally it's about listening to your horse. If your horse shows any discomfort or pain, regardless of what type of bridle... from not wanting to be bridled, to opening their mouths, to looking uncomfortable, then always investigate and do what is best for your horse's health.

When you've got it right for you and your horse - go out, have adventures together and enjoy!

You did it…

Congratulations! You finished this book.

As an equestrian author, book reviews are a valuable way for you to help me share this guide with the world. If you enjoyed this book, I would love it if you could share your review and a photo of this book on your favourite online book store. It will just take a minute or two and I read every review.

Enjoy all my horse books at **www.writtenbyelaine.com**

THE

CONNEMARA
ADVENTURE SERIES
FOR KIDS 8+

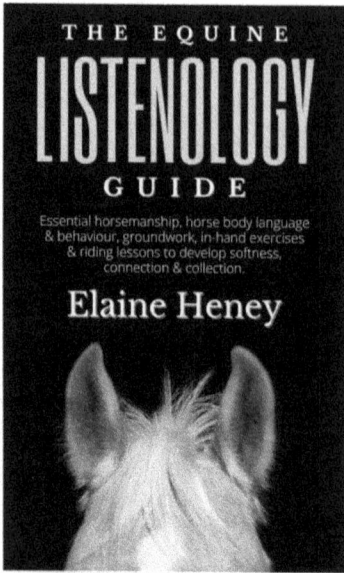

THE EQUINE
LISTENOLOGY
GUIDE

Essential horsemanship, horse body language
& behaviour, groundwork, in-hand exercises
& riding lessons to develop softness,
connection & collection.

Elaine Heney

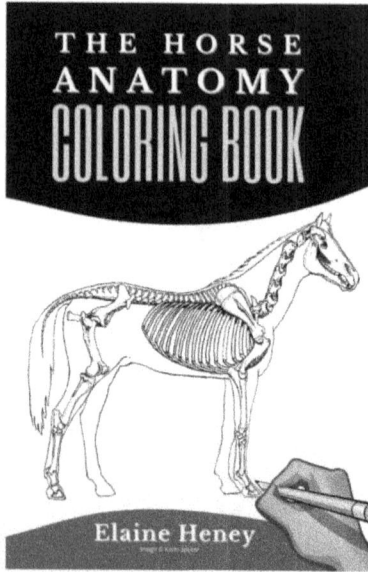

THE HORSE
ANATOMY
COLORING BOOK

Elaine Heney

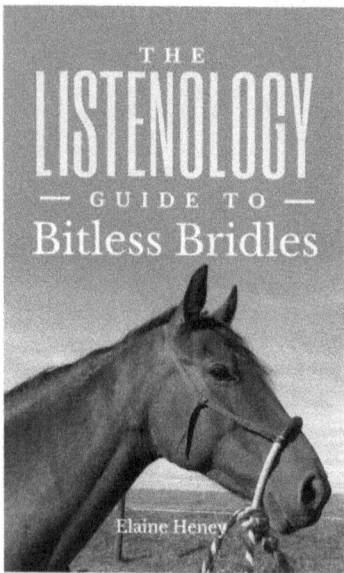

THE
LISTENOLOGY
— GUIDE TO —
Bitless Bridles

Elaine Heney

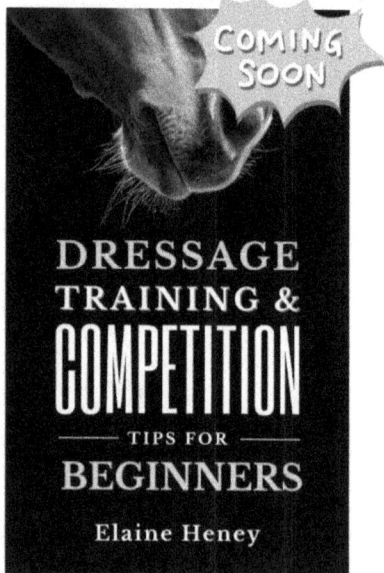

COMING
SOON

DRESSAGE
TRAINING &
COMPETITION
— TIPS FOR —
BEGINNERS

Elaine Heney

EDUCATIONAL HORSE BOOKS FOR KIDS...

www.writtenbyelaine.com

LISTENOLOGY FOR KIDS
The children's guide to horse care, horse body language & behaviour, groundwork, riding & training.
Elaine Heney

HORSE CARE
RIDING AND TRAINING
FOR KIDS
ELAINE HENEY

Horse PUZZLES
Games & Brainteasers
For Kids
With fun horse word puzzles & crosswords!
Elaine Heney

HORSE JOURNAL
FOR KIDS 6-15
Elaine Heney
TRACK YOUR HORSE RIDING LESSONS & HORSE CARE

Online horse training courses

Discover our series of world renowned online groundwork, riding & training programs. Visit Grey Pony Films & learn more:

www.greyponyfilms.com

www.ingramcontent.com/pod-product-compliance
Lightning Source LLC
Chambersburg PA
CBHW071239020426
42333CB00015B/1546